Coming Out Of Cage

Journey of a Tiger Mom
From Tiger Cub to Tiger Mom; Reflection of a Former
School Board Trustee and Education Facilitator

E. Way

WESTBOW·
PRESS
A DIVISION OF THOMAS NELSON
& ZONDERVAN

WestBow Press books may be ordered through
booksellers or by contacting:

WestBow Press
A Division of Thomas Nelson & Zondervan
1663 Liberty Drive
Bloomington, IN 47403
www.westbowpress.com
1 (866) 928-1240

ISBN: 978-1-4908-6653-6 (sc)
ISBN: 978-1-4908-6654-3 (e)

Library of Congress Control Number: 2015900727

Printed in the United States of America.

WestBow Press rev. date: 02/06/2015

Contents

This book is dedicated to my children. Without them, I would not have the motivation, strength, courage, and determination to confront my own baggage from the past and learn to be a person who loves freely and unconditionally.

Introduction

I never thought I was a "Tiger Mom," because I did not think I was domineering or overbearing with my children—principled and firm, maybe, but certainly not unreasonably strict and overly demanding. But to my surprise after being a mom for almost twenty-five years, I came to realize how much of a Tiger Mom I have been to my children, especially my daughter.

Like most parents, I tried to make sure my children got the best education they could. I thought once they were accepted to and left for the colleges of their choice, the toughest part of my job as a parent was done. I never expected the four years my daughter attended college to be even more trying.

Not only was I devastated when I heard from my daughter about the post traumatic stress disorder (PTSD) problem she developed in her first year of college, I was absolutely shocked to find out it had a lot to do with how she was raised. I could not believe much of the pain, pressure, distress, and insecurity she experienced actually came from her father and me, who went our separate ways when she was around nine years old.

To understand what she had to go through and to help her get well, I did all I could, including working with various counselors and therapists, soul-searching, praying, and delving into Bible Scriptures and self-help books. Through the process, my eyes were slowly opened to the many mistakes I made in raising my children.

How I raised my children had a lot to do with how I grew up. Many of my expectations, attitudes, and ways of handling relationships and things in life came from the unresolved fear I experienced since childhood. This fear of not being good enough, failure, punishment, rejection, insignificance, uncertainty, loss, confrontation, and separation caused great insecurity, shame, and guilt. They also generated pride and vain ambition in me. These things trapped me like a cage and drove me to take control of my children's lives.

Never did I imagine I would write a book, especially one that required me to be so transparent and vulnerable. How would people look at me when they found out who I really am behind the facade of success as a community activist, an attorney, an education facilitator and a former elected school board trustee? Would I bring more fear and shame to myself by exposing my innermost thoughts and feelings to the public? I tried to find excuses for not writing this book, but something in me would not stop stirring until I succumbed to its constant nagging.

When I see children hurt by well-meaning and sincerely caring parents like me; students stressed out of shape by the cookie-cutter education system that measures students according to their test scores; families disillusioned by a faulty and failing education system; parents despaired by their children's inability to arrive at an anticipated success level or tormented by their children's struggles with unexpected physical, mental, emotional, and other health issues, I know I have to write this book and share my experiences.

As I went through a healing and reconciliation process, I learned five major lessons.

1) I do not always know what is the best for my children, because I am limited by my inadequacies, shortcomings, and baggage from the past.
2) I have made many mistakes, poor choices, and wrong decisions, and taken improper actions in raising my children. I need to seek forgiveness and establish trust with them.
3) I need to be teachable, patient, ready, and willing to listen to and discover my children's best interests from their standpoints, and help them attain their goals appropriately.
4) I need to be resilient when facing challenges and unceasing in making progress as a parent as well as a person by relying on God's Word and Spirit.
5) Allowing God's love to fill my heart enables me to love my children and others unconditionally and authentically.

This book is not a how-to parenting guidebook. It may, however, offer a mirror for parents to take a closer look at the motives behind their parenting styles and focus. Hopefully, by becoming more aware as to why and how they hold their children to certain expectations, parents will be able to learn to appreciate, respect, trust, and enjoy them more freely and fully.

1

Me, a Tiger Mom?

Tiger Mom: A mother who is overly strict with her child in order to foster an academically competitive spirit. This form of upbringing is intended to direct a child towards financially successful careers at the potential risk of feeling emotionally unfulfilled and/or socially inept.

—*Urban Dictionary*

Tiger Mom: A strict or demanding mother who pushes her children to high levels of achievement, using methods regarded as typical of childrearing in China and other parts of East Asia.

—*Oxford Dictionaries*

Even before my first child was born, I knew I wanted to be the best mom ever. I wanted to do everything I could to protect and provide for my son, so he would be healthy, happy, and successful. So to ensure his well-being even while he was still in my womb,

I played music to stimulate the growth of his brain, kept a nutritious and balanced diet, read numerous parenting manuals, followed my obstetrician's every instruction, and abstained from environments that would be harmful to the fetus. To make sure he would do well throughout his life, I prayed and prayed to God for His blessing and protection. I wanted to be a wise, caring, and understanding mom, capable of providing proper guidance, rich resources, and strong support for my baby.

When my daughter came along two years later, I did the same for her. My heart just leaped with joy at the first sight of her on the ultrasound monitor. Even though the fetus was too little to be identified as a boy or girl, I knew instantly it was a girl from the way she somersaulted and danced in the playground of my womb. I nursed her till she was eleven months old, so I could give her all the nutrients my body could give.

I took pride in making it my priority to constantly provide support and to take care of my children's needs. I also followed the wise Chinese teaching - 讀萬卷書不如行萬里路 — *du- wan-juan-shu-bu-ru-xing-wan-li-lu* - "reading ten thousand books does not compare to traveling ten thousand miles" by taking my children on regular family trips to broaden their horizons.

Like many parents, I searched all possible afterschool lessons and weekend programs. I tried to fill my kids' schedules during school breaks with activities that were available and affordable, arranged extracurricular activities to enrich their learning experiences, advanced them by one grade level when opportunities were available, supported their placements in GATE programs, and helped them develop their potentials by exposing them to all kinds of educational opportunities. I did not want my kids to miss out or be left behind in any way.

In no way did I think the tennis, swimming, and piano lessons; summer camps; Chinese schools; math and science enrichment programs; church clubs and activities... I arranged for them were excessive or unreasonable. I thought I was doing everything responsible and loving parents do for their children. In no way did I think I was domineering and overbearing, in short, a Tiger Mom.

Imagine my shock when my daughter disclosed lots of the heartrending experiences she suffered while growing up. What a blow that was to my ego and pride! I thought I was a great mom. How could I have caused her so much hurt and anguish that she developed PTSD after entering college?

I was forced to examine my parenting approach to see if I had done anything to contribute to this disorder. Did I put my daughter into too many activities against her will and interest? Did the separation of her father and me cause her too much anxiety and frustration? Was I too busy and inattentive to her state of mind when she was growing up? Did I objectify her and treat her like a project that needed to be fixed? Did I dictate her life without considering her individuality? Did I deprive her of opportunities to take charge of her life by hovering over her too much and jumping in to offer unsolicited assistance?

After many futile attempts to justify my parenting practices, I came to terms with the fact I had indeed messed up in many ways as a parent. I had essentially been a Tiger Mom to my children when I imposed my expectations on them without checking whether such expectations met their true interests. I often did what I thought was good for them out of my own convenience, pride, and needs. When my children tried to tell me their thoughts and feelings, I tended to listen selectively and only hear what met with my approval or schedule. I often effectively disregarded my children's interests and perspectives. Just because they complied and seldom complained about the plans I made for them did not mean they enjoyed or appreciated them. My children were often afraid to speak up because they did not want me to get mad at or be disappointed in them.

To understand what made me such a Tiger Mom, I decided to look back at my childhood. It was terribly trying. I had to look deep into my heart, honestly explore my own growing-up process, and intently confront my past in order to own up to some painful realities. Yet I am thankful because this endeavor allowed me to face up to the fear, insecurity, pride, self-righteousness, guilt, and shame that for many years held me captive.

Things to Think About:

- Do you think you might also be a Tiger parent?
- Do you always look for opportunities to help your children excel and work hard to ensure happy lives and successful futures for them?

- Do you feel easily let down when your children do not live up to your expectations?
- Do you feel hurt and consider your children ungrateful when they do not show appreciation for your hard work?
- Do you feel competitive toward other families and easily jealous or envious when other kids seem to do better than your kids?

2

Living in a Cage of Fear

> Fear can be a trap, but if you trust in the Lord,
> you will be safe.
>
> —Proverbs 29:25 (ERV)

Fear is a powerful feeling. It can immobilize us, keep us from doing what we ought to do, and drive us to do what we should not do. Fear is not simply the lack of courage and peace; it is often the absence of love and faith. When we give in to fear, whether real or perceived, rational or irrational, we are essentially living in a cage and kept in bondage.

I walk my dog every day. There is one path that he hesitates to travel because there are often two big German shepherds lounging behind the barred gate of a house on that street. These two dogs are quite well trained, and they have never come too close to my dog. However, my dog is frightened of them because he was attacked by another German shepherd a few years ago when we walked by its house. I have tried to coax my dog by telling him not to be scared of the two dogs because they have no power over him, but my dog will not stop panicking. Not only does he lack courage and feel antsy whenever he comes in the vicinity of these two big dogs, he also does not trust my love and ability to protect him from them.

This is a typical case of what the Chinese call— 一朝被蛇咬,十年怕井繩 - *yi-zhao-bei-she-yao, shi-nian-pa-jing-sheng*, which literally means once bitten by a snake, the sight of a rope will cause fright for ten years.

Like my dog, I have experienced incidents that have caused lingering fear and have scarred and debilitated me. However, unlike my dog, who shows his fear unabashedly, I have suppressed my fear because I see it as a sign of weakness and vulnerability. It is also embarrassing to mention and would likely make listeners feel uneasy. I have coped with fear passively and secretly, thereby giving fear control of my mind. I, in turn, have become its prisoner.

I attended highly prestigious, private, Chinese grade and middle schools in Taiwan. Like most of the other Chinese schools at the time, they practiced severe disciplinary measures, including shaming and corporal punishment. Teachers had the authority to punish students for whatever reason and by whatever means. So if students misbehaved in class, did not turn in homework, got low test scores or bad grades, ate or talked without permission, forgot to bring homework or any required school items (such as a handkerchief), wore an untidy or mismatched uniform, and so on, they could be punished. Some teachers scolded them relentlessly in front of the class, made them kneel on the hard cement floor, spanked them with freshly cut bamboo sticks, slapped them in the face, hit them on the head, pulled their hair, or made them write repentance notes hundreds of times.

Good grades and high test scores were everything. They defined a student as smart and worthy. Whenever the test scores and school grades were announced publicly, I cringed. To me, as long as I was in the top 45 percent in a class of sixty students, I was safe. I remember getting sixth place in second grade once. My mom was so happy she bought special treats for everyone in the class. I was so happy to have made my parents proud!

This fear of public humiliation, corporal punishment, mockery, shame, rejection, and failure that I developed at an early age made me feel as though trapped. This feeling was fortified by the culture and tradition in which I was raised, and it prompted me to study hard and do well in school.

I am certain many of my classmates and my siblings also suffered from this fear. No one talked about it, however, because it was an integral part of our culture and education system. Being punished or humiliated at school was so common no one thought it was improper. I heard parents give teachers specific requests and permission to spank their kids because they sincerely believed in 棒打出孝子 —*bang-da-chu-xiao-zi*—meaning hitting with a rod makes a virtuous and obedient child.

As a child, I fantasized about having the ability to fly. I wished I could fly as fast, as far, and as high as I could, especially in view of an imminent chastisement from a teacher or grown-up. I desired freedom from the fear of being punished, stigmatized, and debased. I wished I could escape from all the authorities inherent in the education and social system. Yet I dared not tread beyond the institutionalized norms, because while they kept me imprisoned, they also gave me a structure of life and framework of mind.

I knew as long as I stayed within the confinement of the educational system's cage, abide by the protocols to do well academically, and follow the proper code of conduct, I would be protected from reproach. I did not want to take risks or stand out in any odd fashion, lest I got in trouble or be accused as being dumb, lazy, peculiar, or show-offish. I studied mainly to get by and to give the appearance of being competent and even accomplished. It was not so much for the purpose of getting real knowledge, especially since I did not even find many of the topics relevant or interesting!

There were a few occasions when the creative flames in me flickered, but they were quickly snuffed out. I learned from these experiences that I should not even try to be innovative; I must comply and conform.

Once I composed a simple melody on piano. I excitedly shared it with my music teacher. Her only response was, "Hmmm, it sounds familiar to me. Did you come up with it yourself?" Her cold and terse remark took away all my confidence and desire to compose. She was apparently telling me I was incapable of writing music and most likely copying somebody else's work.

Another time I tried to draw a scene I saw in the movie *Planet of the Apes*, starring Charlton Heston (my hero!). It was for an in-class painting assignment. When I messed up the painting, I decided to paint the paper all black and just outline the scene against the black background, so I would not waste the paper. My art teacher gave me an F. I gathered enough courage to explain to him I used the black background to show how dark the world would be when it fell into the hands of apes. Even though he gave me a passing grade, I felt mortified about the very low score. Again, I thought it was wrong to think outside the box!

While I was average in my elementary-class ranking, I was an excellent singer. It was such an honor for me to represent my class in a singing competition once. I totally bombed it though, because fear and anxiety incapacitated me during the competition. I simply could not find my voice to hit the high notes. The messages, *Who do you think you are? What makes you think you will have a chance to win? You are never good enough to win anything; you are just making a fool out of yourself,* kept playing in my head. I remember feeling extreme shame and guilt for losing, and I wished I had never entered the contest.

Things to Think About:

- Do you find yourself living in a cage?
- What kind of cage is it?

- Do you find yourself hiding in the cage because it is easier to continue living with what is familiar and safer to maintain the status quo?
- What is your fear? Is it fear of failure, shame, illness, pain, death, dark, deception, rejection, attack, danger, intimacy, abandonment, loneliness, insignificance, ridicules, separation, poverty, uncertainties, unknown, chaos, commitment, mess, abandonment, or something else?
- Does your fear drive you to success, or does it paralyze you to inaction or dysfunction?
- Are you raising your children out of a fear they will not succeed, be unhappy, get hurt, get depressed, lose out, miss out, be attacked, be bullied, be endangered, get addicted, and so on?
- Are you raising your children out of a fear that you might be labeled as a substandard parent?

3

Growing Up as a Tiger Cub

虎父無犬子 - Tiger Father, Tiger Son
—Chinese Proverb

The Chinese culture in which I grew up highly esteemed the value of honoring parents and pursuing an excellent education. Since my dad was born in the year of Tiger, and my mom considered herself a Tiger Girl because she was the daughter of a prominent two-star general, I naturally took pride in being a Tiger Cub. After all, Tiger Father breeds Tiger Cub -*虎父無犬子*— *hu-fu-wu-quan-zi*—which literally means no child of a strong Tiger Dad would be a wimpy puppy! Growing up as a Tiger Cub, and the oldest of four children in my family, I strived to live up to my parents' expectations by doing well academically and leading my younger siblings by example.

My parents worked hard to provide the best education for us. Like many Chinese parents, they followed the exemplary model of the mother of Mencius - *孟子*—*Meng-Zi*, a famous philosopher on a par with Confucius - *孔子*—*Kung-Zi*. Mencius's mother -*孟*

母—*Meng- Mu*, has been highly admired and emulated by many Chinese parents because of what she did for the education of her son. She was best known for孟 母三遷 — *Meng-Mu-san-qian* - moving three times, to settle Mencius at a site where quality and essential education was available and accessible to him. Like Mencius's mom, my parents moved our family to a neighborhood where the best school was located when I was starting kindergarten. When I was in high school, my parents went through countless obstacles to move us to California that, in their opinion, offered the best education at that time.

Education as the ultimate key to success in life was profoundly ingrained in my mind. I firmly believed that without a good education, I would not be able to get a good job; without a good job, I would not be able to find a good spouse and have a good marriage; without a good marriage, I would not be able to raise good children and build a good family. Such was my culture and upbringing. In this culture, not only would the students who got good grades be considered smart, they would also be looked upon as better looking and superior in all other aspects. So not only did good grades determine a person's worth, they also impacted his or her self-worth. How we viewed ourselves had a lot to do with how others labeled us.

An incident during my second grade could not be erased from my mind, because it made me feel so worthless and shameful, like a culprit who deserved to vanish from the face of the earth. One day I saw my mom on the school campus, talking to my teacher. I was surprised to see her and asked her why she came to my school. She said because I misbehaved in class, my teacher called her to come to school, so my teacher could spank her hand. I had no clue what I did that called for a spanking, but I took my mom's word for it and felt immensely guilty and remorseful. I wished I could disappear because surely everyone had heard about the terrible thing I did to make my mom pay for my penalty. A few days later, I found out she was just joking with me, but it affected me so much I started to develop a strong guilt conscience. I swore I would never put my parents through any punishment on account of me again.

Since I was slightly overweight when I was in grade school, people made fun of me. I was terribly troubled whenever we had to be weighed at the nurse's office. Each kid had to get on the scale to have his or her weight checked. The number was announced so it could be recorded. As far as I could remember, I always weighed 10kg. (approximately 22 pounds) more than the girl next to me, who was the same height as I was. This girl also happened to be the smartest girl because she always got the highest grade point average and ranked number one in my class!

I found myself unwilling to go to the clothes tailors with my mom and siblings when I was little. Influenced by the movie *The Sound of Music,* my mom wanted all three of her daughters to wear dresses of the same design, as if wearing a school uniform six days a week was not enough! I was very upset every time I saw the embroidered markings on the inside of my dress.

Since I was the oldest and the biggest of the three girls, the word "大 - *da*—large" was always embroidered in my dress. It just seemed extra-large to me every time I looked at it. I felt humungous and absurd looking.

People also made fun of my headful of frizzy hair when I was young. Unlike most Chinese girls, with nice, long naturally straight, black hair, I had thick, frizzy, permed, dark brownish, short hair. My mom had a very difficult time trying to comb through my hair after washing it each time. I always felt guilty for putting her through so much work!

To match my weird hairdo, I had a mouthful of braces, with little rubber bands tied to them. Wearing braces was such an unusual thing more than forty years ago. As far as I can remember, I was the only one in the entire fourth grade who wore braces! I dreaded the possibility that I would never be socially acceptable.

There is a saying I heard long time ago from some source I do not remember. It applies aptly to how I thought of myself.

> You are not who you think you are,
> You are not who others think you are,
> You are who you think others might think
> you are.

My identity was pretty much based on my belief of how other people looked at me. Such a projected view defined and shaped how I coped with people and circumstances. Perceiving myself as the child who bore the highest expectations from my parents, I assumed a superior, authoritative, and arrogant demeanor toward my brother and sisters. Yet seeing myself as plain and mediocre from the viewpoints of my teachers and classmates, I kept low-keyed and stayed away from trouble. So while I was pushy toward my siblings, I was withdrawn from my classmates.

This interesting dynamic between the two identities—one that drove me to take control and seek the limelight and the other that made me resist attention and retreat to the background—worked to cultivate a fight-or-flight attitude. As long as I was convinced I was well regarded, I would fight to excel to keep up with the image of respectability and even superiority. As soon as I felt belittled, however, I would flee, hide, and keep a safe distance. This fight-or-flight attitude pretty much governed the way I handled many relationships and commitments in life.

Despite my tendency to run from difficult people and troublesome situations, I never stopped bearing the responsibilities I was taught and trained to take on as I was growing up because they had been deeply built into my character. In addition to the duty to lead by example that my mom commanded me by saying, "There are only six of us in our family. You are the oldest after your dad and me, and we expect you to set good example for your sisters and brother to follow," there was also the 四維八德 – (si-wei-ba-de – "Code of Four Disciplines and Eight Virtues") I was taught at school — 禮 (li – "respect, propriety"), 義 ("yi – "justice"), 廉 (lian—"honesty, integrity"), 恥 (chi—"honor, humility"); 忠 (zhong - "loyalty"), 孝 (xiao - "filial piety"), 仁 (*ren*—"humanity"), 愛 (*ai*—"compassion"), 信 (*xin*—"trustworthiness"), 義 (*yi*—"righteousness"), 和 (*he*—"unity"), and 平 (*ping*—"peace, harmony").

Whatever I did, I wanted to bring honor to my parents and win their approval, as well as hold myself out as a decent human being and good citizen to honor my culture, heritage, and ancestry. The fear of causing any disgrace served as an impetus for many of the choices I made in life. The fear of causing disappointment prompted me to work hard to attain high achievements and respectable status in life.

I am by no means criticizing my parents by alluding to some of the past occurrences. I know they meant well and never intended to hurt me in any way. The older I get, the more I understand how challenging life must have been for them—living through the Sino-Japanese War, escaping communism to make a new life in Taiwan, trying to build a small nuclear family while maintaining an extended large family structure, and raising four children born within two years. I also understand why they expected so much out of me as their oldest child.

They were truly avant-garde by moving my siblings and me all the way across the Pacific Ocean to California forty years ago to give us the best learning opportunities they could find at the time. To give us a chance to excel, they also had to endure physical separation from each other for many years. Our mom stayed in California to take care of us, while our dad continuing to work overseas to pay the bills.

Things to Think About:

- Do you have childhood memories, experiences, and trainings that shape your way of thinking and living?
- Do you find yourself trying hard to please your parents and make them proud?
- Do you feel guilty when you think you have failed to live up to your parents' expectations?
- Have you felt you would never be good enough for your parents?
- Do you abide by a code of conduct and virtues?
- Are you passing this code of honor and discipline on to your children and instilling traditional and cultural values in them?

4

Cage within a Cage

People are slaves to whatever has mastered them.

—2 Peter 2:19 (NIV)

Surely you know that you become the slaves of whatever you give yourselves to. Anything or anyone you follow will be your master.

—Romans 6:16 (ERV)

Coming to California might have been the ultimate American dream for many overseas families forty years ago, but it was a nightmare for me. My parents were not aware of the traumatic impact the move to California had on me because they were too busy adapting themselves. At the sensitive and impressionable age of fifteen, friends were everything to me. It was terribly devastating for me to leave all my friends behind, especially since we had no means to stay in touch with each other except by writing letters, which would take at least a week to deliver, or by making phone calls, which was outrageously expensive! The song *"Please Mr. Postman"* amply described my state of mind at the time and kept me company for many long, lonely days.

Adding to the challenges of learning the English language, I had to adjust to a brand-new life in America. I was horrified when I found myself attending a big high school in the middle of a school year. There were about three thousand students in this high school, and everyone looked so big and tall to me. Hardly any Chinese or Asians were in this school. I was probably the only overseas-born Chinese until my younger sister was promoted to ninth grade a few months later. I felt ugly, small, stupid, pathetic, and lonely.

I did not dare tell my mom about my frustrations and fear, because it would only add to her burden. My mom was pretty much a single mom because she had to take care of four teenagers without our dad around. I, being the oldest child, felt obligated to share her load. Without having anyone to turn to, I turned to food for comfort and ended up having an eating disorder.

Not many people knew what an eating disorder was about at that time, least of all me. All I wanted to do was lose some weight so that I would look more attractive and be more likable. I started by starving myself and felt proud when I began to thin down. People began to notice me more and paid me compliments for looking prettier. However, it did not stop there. I went from not eating to compulsive eating. I knew something was wrong with me, but I did not know what. Trying to look up the medical dictionaries in the school library did not help, since eating disorder was not even a medical condition in those days, and the terms "anorexia nervosa" and "bulimia" were not in the medical dictionaries—assuming I knew there were the conditions I should look up, which I didn't. I could not tell my mom about it or consult with anyone, because I thought no one would understand or be able to help, but they would only be worried and nervous. I essentially lived a double life by acting normal in front of people, but binging-purging behind them in secret. I lived a double life in front and behind people, and I felt exceedingly disgusted and shameful, but I could not stop. It became a vicious cycle. The more I binged, the more depressed I got, and the more depressed I got, the more I binged.

It never occurred to me that I would have an addiction problem, because I had always been self-disciplined and never allowed myself to take on any harmful habit like smoking, drinking alcohol, or doing drugs. The tricky thing about my eating disorder was that it did not seem harmful initially, and it could be covered up easily. When I started to exercise strict control over the intake of food and lose a lot of weight, I was ecstatic and proud of the fruit of my discipline.

I did not expect my self-control to turn around and take control of me. This seemingly effective and harmless weight control measure started to bite me once I took a bite of it. It quickly became a way of life for me because it was comforting and familiar. It gave me a sense of security and structure, even though it was destructive by nature. It was also an escape for me. By numbing myself with food, I could avoid dealing with many issues I did not want to face. I got trapped in this cage of addictive eating when I tried to escape from the cage of fear of rejection and dejection. It was a cage within a cage, and I kept it a secret for fifteen years. It is truly a wonder to me that I did not die because of it.

Things to Think About:

- Have you ever suffered any addiction problems?
- Do you know what led you to the addiction(s)?
- Have you, in an effort to become successful, found yourself roped into some habits and behavior patterns that will enslave you?
- Have you experienced any deep shame that seemed to be beyond pardon and restoration?
- Do you have wise friends or mentors in life you could trust and turn to for guidance and support?

5

Living a Facade of Success

For if anyone thinks he is something, when he
is nothing, he deceives himself.
—Galatians 6:3 (NIV)

To disguise my fear, insecurity, guilt, and shame, I
tried to put on the look of success, strength, power,
and achievement, like the great and powerful Wizard
of Oz, who hid his smallness and plainness behind
magic tricks and special effects. To honor my parents
and make them proud, I pursued a BA degree from Cal
Berkeley and a JD law degree from the University of
San Francisco. Then I passed the California Bar exam
and became an attorney.

When it was the right time for marriage and family,
I married a hardworking Chinese man who shared
similar cultural values and education background,
worked with him to build a family business, and
raised two wonderful children. Miraculously, when I
got pregnant with my first child, I was able to stop the
fifteen-year binging-purging cycle without any medical

or psychological help. The love I had for this new life in me enabled me to quit the habit instantaneously and effortlessly. To me, my baby far surpassed the importance of the eating habit, and I did not want to jeopardize his health in any way. I was totally freed from the eating problem. No more shame of living a double life. No more secret!

Two years later, my beautiful baby girl came along. With the arrival of the healthy babies, the security of marriage, and a flourishing family business, I felt blessed and blissful, as if I were on cloud nine. The Chinese word for "good"—好—*hao* is made up of a son -子—*zi* and a daughter -女—*nuu*. Having a son and daughter is regarded a very good thing. Not only did I bring honor to my parents, I brought honor to my husband and his parents. Respect and appreciation were shown me from everyone in the family and circles of friends.

People complimented me for being such a good helpmate to my husband. They said I was the Wings to a Tiger —如虎添翼— *ru-hu-tian-yi*. I was so elated that I prided myself, thinking I had earned the badge of a Proverbs 31 (NIV) Woman of Noble Character, whose, "husband has full confidence in her," and who, "brings him good, not harm all the days of her life … provides food for her family, … sets about her work vigorously, … opens her arms to the poor and extends her hands to the needy, … is clothed with strength and dignity, … speaks with wisdom, … her children arise and call her blessed, her husband also, and he praises her."

However, this utopia did not last long. As our family business expanded, conflict between my husband and me also worsened. I had to quit working with him. By doing so, our sixteen-year marital relationship was also stopped.

In a way, it was a self-fulfilling prophecy that our marriage failed. I remember when I was a toddler, maybe around two years old at the time, my parents took me to YangMingShan National Park with many relatives one day. Someone won a tiny, plastic, magenta-colored toy clipped purse at a ring toss game and gave it to me. I remember really loving that little purse and was heartbroken when I found it in the big cage of our two German shepherd dogs a few days later. The little purse was all chewed up! This memory somehow left me with the impression I did not deserve to have anything good, and good things simply would not last.

The broken marriage crushed me and made me feel discarded and worthless. While my food addiction was a hidden and private shame, my broken marriage was an open and public disgrace. Not only did I dishonor my parents, I hurt my kids, and disappoint many friends and loved ones. I felt like a social outcast with the word "shame" written large and in bold all over my face. Therefore, I should wear a brown bag over my head wherever I went.

Just as I was going through the lowest point of my life, an opportunity to run for the local school board came to me. I was so flattered that people would actually consider asking and promoting me for such an important position. The security of home and family business that I lost was replaced by the support of people who rallied around me to campaign for the local school board trustee position. I had no idea what the school board was about, what a school board trustee should do, or how to run a campaign, but I relished the attention and prospect of becoming prominent because I so desperately needed a way out of the cage of shame of a failed marriage.

To show my parents I could attain significance even as an unmarried woman, to secure myself with a distinguished title as an elected official, and to assure my children I would not be defeated by setbacks in life, I put on the appearance of confidence and strength as I sailed through the campaign process. I was elected to serve on the school board of a fairly large public school district in 2004, and in 2008, I was reelected to a second term. What brought me exceeding gratitude and joy was to have my parents with me at my campaign kickoff in 2004 and at the swearing-in ceremony in 2008.

As soon as I got elected, I endeavored to learn the school board trade quickly. I developed a sociopolitical life that demanded a lot of my time and energy. With school board meetings at least twice a month, and each meeting lasting an average of seven hours and sometimes ten hours, it was not possible for me to spend a lot of time with my children. I justified my busyness by thinking it was a necessary and worthwhile sacrifice for a bigger good, and my children would be proud to see their mother overseeing not only their schools but all forty-two schools in their school district.

As one of the few Chinese elected officials, I had the opportunity to represent our school community at various important functions and meet high-profiled politicians and dignitaries. I felt distinguished whenever I was introduced as a VIP or honorable guest. I got a significant amount of media and attention and even collected a few prestigious awards and recognitions in the few years I served. Convincing myself that my parents and children should be proud of me because of my contributions to society, I was, in fact, feeding my selfish ego and ambition, which was as insatiate as it was fleeting, vain, and empty. I was in truth pursuing and living a facade.

Things to Think About:

- Do you tend to put work before family and material success before relationships?
- Do you catch yourself being so drawn to fame, success, and power that you lose sight of the real priorities in life?
- Are there people in your life who know you well and care about you enough to hold you accountable in setting proper priorities and boundaries in life?

6

Exposing the Facade

Are there any among you who are really wise and understanding? Then you should show your wisdom by living right. You should do what is good with humility. A wise person does not boast. If you are selfish and have bitter jealousy in your hearts, you have no reason to boast. Your boasting is a lie that hides the truth.

—James 3:13, 14 (ERV)

Decorating the cage with fancy titles and accolades could not eradicate the underlying fear I suffered since childhood and shame I endured from the broken marriage. Trying to disguise them with a facade of success was like covering up a stench with perfume. The core problem festers and gets worse if not addressed timely and properly.

In 2007, a year after my divorce petition was filed, I was diagnosed with breast cancer. This unexpected news brought me new fears of growing old-ill-feeble, losing womanhood, and maybe even becoming an invalid and dependent one day. It was sobering for me to see how fragile I could easily become. Without getting any conclusive finding as to the cause of my cancer, I could only surmise it was due to stress over the divorce and school board challenges.

With the diagnosis and treatment of breast cancer, this facade behind which I tried to hide my inner struggles started to peel off a little. Even though outwardly I was hanging on strong by surviving cancer and beating other adversities in life, inwardly I felt trapped in an aging and deteriorating body, as well as institutionalized in a downward spiraling dysfunctional social-political-educational system.

After working on the school board for eight years, I could see how many politicians and special interest groups abused the system for their own purposes, how some public servants who started out with altruistic goals to serve the community turned greedy and self-aggrandizing, and how organizations and individuals often played games to elevate themselves and their causes at the expense of other people. The ugliness of getting ahead, getting big, and getting more at all costs, without considering others' interests and values, drove me to an utter disgust with the system. Above all, I was mostly disgusted with myself for coveting fame, power, and glory, just like many others!

When I visited high school classes, I liked to tell students little stories to help them better understand my point of view. One of the illustrations I gave was found in a book I read long time ago – *Hope for the Flowers* by Trina Paulus. It was about a little caterpillar who aimed to climb high by stepping all over others and pushing them out of his way. When he managed to get to the top, he found out that he really wasted a lot of time and effort like millions of other caterpillars, because there was nothing up there! He could have flown up without hurting anyone at all, had he followed the course of his natural life patiently, diligently and faithfully! He would be able to find love and become a butterfly to bring seeds of love from heaven to earth and spread them among flowers.

Like the little caterpillar, I had been so caught up in the trends to aim high and race to the top that I lost sight of the true purpose of my being. The titles and honors I worked hard to acquire became a farce once I saw the emptiness in all these pursuits. They were like the colorful feathers a crow collected from birds of other species and glued to its body in hope of transforming itself into an ultrasplendid bird! The feathers only made the crow look foolish and absurd. When the wind and rain came, all the feathers were blown off. The crow worked hard for nothing!

Being able to see the facade for what it was gave me a sense of freedom. It allowed me to take off the mask to face my vulnerable self honestly, and to get on with my life more meaningfully and peacefully. As I often told students, "Be the best you that you can be because nobody else can out you, you." I am finally learning to apply my own teaching to my walk in life.

Things to Think About:

- Do you feel you have to prove your worth to other people?
- Do you define success as gaining titles, credentials and fame as well as accumulating wealth and power?
- Do you find wearing designer clothing, using name-brand products, attending renowned schools, joining prestigious clubs, associating with reputable organizations, etc. somehow enhance your worth?
- Do you find yourself climbing up a ladder to who knows where?
- Do you feel empty despite all your achievements in life?

7

8 Specific Parenting Mistakes

Hurt People, Hurt People.

—Sandra Wilson

The fear that empowered me to live the facade of successful life also ensnared me to blunder my parenting in multiple ways. I made several specific mistakes in raising my children, which could have been avoided had I realized how much a Tiger Mom I was and had I found out what drove me to be a Tiger Mom sooner. These mistakes had a stronger impact on my daughter than my son because they were often reactions toward my daughter when I found her falling short of the standard of achievement and performance set by my son.

Mistake #1: Expecting My Children to Perform Equally Well Despite Their Differences

One mistake I made was to assume whatever was good for my son would also be just as good for my daughter. Without considering their differences in age, capabilities, interests, and personalities, I signed up both children for the same activities and programs, albeit at different levels. I thought it would be fair to offer my daughter what was offered to my son and that my daughter would enjoy the activities just as much and perform just as well as my son. I also did it out of convenience because I would only need to devise one set of plans for both kids.

Since my daughter was younger and not able to learn as quickly as her brother when she was little, she had to put in more effort. Her brother often overshadowed her not only by setting high standards that were difficult for her to follow but also by winning my confidence more easily because we were more like-minded and tended to work at similar pace.

My inconsiderateness of the differences between my children, and unrealistic expectation to hold them to the same level of performance, often made my daughter feel inadequate and insecure.

Mistake #2: Comparing My Children to Each Other

I was also wrong to compare my children to each other, consciously and subconsciously. By pointing out their strengths and weaknesses to each other, I was hoping they would have more incentive to do better, but it caused needless strife.

My daughter's handwriting and drawing were better than her brother's. She was able to print and write beautifully, even while she was in kindergarten. However, to perfect her handwriting even more, she became so uptight and nervous in holding a pencil that she could not even write properly for a while.

By comparing my children to each other, not only did I promote sibling rivalry between them, I also helped to condition them in the roles they should play. While my son was expected to play the role of the big brother and continually take the lead and set the example, my daughter was held to a more subordinate role as a follower. To prove her worth and strength, my daughter drove herself really hard and adopted a perfectionist attitude.

Mistake #3: Encouraging an Unrealistic Standard of Perfection

Although I could see how overly self-critical my daughter was and how prone she was toward perfectionism, I did not consider it a vice. I actually thought her motivation to aim for excellence was commendable, even though I could see how unrealistic some of her aspirations were, given her age and level of maturity. Instead of teaching her to be content and thankful, I encouraged her to be impractical by stepping in to help her whenever I saw her struggling to attain that lofty goal of perfection.

I thought my giving her a hand was helping her build self-confidence, but it only gave her a false sense of accomplishment. She was not able to enjoy herself or be pleased with the result, even if the desired standard was attained, because she would always see the flaws. As a parent, I should have been more discerning in how to guide my child and not reinforce an elusive goal that would lead to unnecessary discouragement and defeat.

Mistake #4: Accelerating My Children's Growth

Good intention does not make good parenting. Advancing my children by allowing them to skip grades and occasionally assisting them on school projects actually did them a disservice. It robbed them of the opportunity to learn more in depth and details at their own pace.

This could be compared to the stifling of a caterpillar's transformation. By cracking open the cocoon before its time and not allowing it to go through the full term of metamorphosis, a butterfly's life would be stunted and deformed.

In my endeavor to boost my daughter's confidence, I did what the Chinese would call 揠苗助長—*ya-miao-zhu-zhang*— pull the plant shoot up to accelerate its growth. It might give her the appearance of growth, but it kept her from maturing naturally. Further, by offering her unsolicited assistance, I was basically impressing on her that I did not trust her to be capable of taking care of herself.

Mistake #5: Mindlessly Saying Foolish and Hurtful Things

My daughter overheard me say to my son in Chinese that she was useless—沒有用—*mei-you-yong*—behind her back once. I had no recollection as to why or under what context I made such injurious comment that badly crippled her self-worth. The hurtful words were spoken like spilled milk. I could not take them back.

I also called her remorseless once for something she did that I cannot remember either. Again, she was very young at the time and felt voiceless to defend herself. So she simply absorbed these damaging words and allowed them to label her.

Even though I did not mean to hurt her, and very likely said these horrible things out of frustration or impatience at the time, it was not excusable. I should not have put her down under any circumstances. As taught in Colossians 3:21 (NIV), we as parents should *"not embitter [our] children, or they will become discouraged."*

Mistake #6: Making Major Decisions without Considering the Impact on My Children

When my daughter was ready for junior high school, I decided to transfer her from the private K–12 school to a top-ranked, public, junior high school with many high-achieving students. Seeing how well my son was able to transition to the high-performing, public school system, I thought it would also be good to transfer my daughter. This change uprooted her from a familiar school environment, where she thrived and had many friends. She managed to adjust to the new school and completed the two challenging school years with overall ease, academic-wise. However, emotionally, she was battling to make sense of all the fast changes within and around her.

Another major decision was made between her father and me about our family structure. Even though the agreement to move forward with a divorce was necessary and mutual, it should have been done more discreetly and prudently. It was very untimely and unfortunate that the court hearing was scheduled for the morning on the same day as our daughter's eighth grade promotion. As she walked with her class to the school yard where the promotion ceremony took place that day, she was put through extra agony when she saw her parents standing on the opposite sides of the field as two total strangers!

Our children might be too young to understand many decisions we make, but if the outcome of the decisions will have a direct impact on them, they should be included in the process, so they have an opportunity to express their thoughts. Depriving them that opportunity only makes them feel voiceless and helpless, as well as angry and frustrated.

Mistake #7: Burdening the Children with Personal Trials

As a family, we should always be able to share our joys, sorrows, likes, dislikes, successes, failures, hopes, dreams, opinions, and other sentiments with each other honestly and trustingly as a way to show love, give support, and strengthen family unity. However, as a mother, I should be cautious in not over-communicating information, especially things that subject my children to excessive and needless burdens.

While I was going through divorce, I talked about some of my pain and grief with my children because I wanted their understanding and forgiveness. I tried to explain the situation to them as calmly and objectively as I could, so it would not bring unnecessary confusion and animosity. But my face and tone of voice could not hide my hurt, resentment, sadness, fear, shame, and guilt. My children were put in the awkward position of feeling responsible for my well-being and to look after me. They were just teenagers.

A few months after the divorce petition was filed, I was diagnosed with breast cancer. It was a total surprise to me because for years, I had been told by my doctor that I was "disgustingly healthy," and I did not detect anything wrong with my body.

This news deepened my children's sense of responsibility toward me. My sixteen-year-old son was working on his college applications at the time. He managed to stay calm and focused, and completed the college application procedures timely. However, instead of aiming for the Ivy League, he set his goal on attending a local university so that he could be close by to take care of his sister and me. My daughter had more difficulty coping with this news because it added to the instability and insecurity she was already enduring. Knowing her brother would soon be leaving home for college further exacerbated her fear and anxiety. Not only was she worried about her chance of getting breast cancer one day, she also worried that the responsibility to take care of me would fall on her shoulders.

There is a common Chinese saying, 養兒防老—*yang-er-fang-lao*, which means raising children so that you will have someone to take care of you in your old age. I always shunned this mind-set because I never wanted to burden my children by making them responsible for my old age. Yet, by sharing some of my personal trials with my children, I laid such an expectation on them.

Mistake #8: Meddling with My Children's Lives

As soon as my daughter got into high school at the age of thirteen, she tried out for the girls' tennis team. She was so happy when she made the first cut. But on the day of the second try-out, she learned she had scoliosis, and her doctor advised her not to play tennis anymore. Her dream to join the team shattered. As a teenager, she wanted to look pretty and be accepted by her peers, but she had to wear a bulky back brace to school every day and use a wheeled backpack, while other kids looked cool and carried regular backpacks.

Her scoliosis could not be corrected, despite seeing a few spinal specialists and chiropractors, because of the irregular shape of one vertebrae. A major spinal surgery was needed to keep her back from bending further. During the summer break before her senior year in high school, she went through a six-hour surgery. Two titanium rods were placed in her spine, leaving a fourteen-inch, zigzagged scar on her back. Students mocked her when she put on weight because she was not able to get much exercise after the surgery.

I was so fraught with guilt, thinking it was my fault she had scoliosis. I wanted to make up for it however I could. To help her rise above her circumstances, I found myself excessively and compulsively meddling with her life. I wanted to make sure my daughter would be able to get into a good college, as my son had, so I sought out ways to help her. My unsolicited advice and assistance hugely undermined, disturbed, and confused my daughter because I kept getting in her way and interfering with her plans.

In my mind, I was helping her get what she wanted. In reality, I was helping her get what I wanted for her. If she failed to get into a good college, it would reflect poorly on me as a parent. I did not want to be looked upon as an inadequate mom, especially since I already failed as a wife and since I was serving as a school board trustee who was highly regarded as an authority on education by many in our school community.

Things to Think About:

- Do you know what your children are really thinking, feeling, or doing? What fears and struggles do they face in school, at play, home, or elsewhere?
- Do you know what outlet your children find to alleviate their fears, frustrations, and worries?
- Do you sense any void and emptiness in your children?
- Do you try to fill that void in your children with material things, like toys, games, high-tech gadgets, electronic devices, money, and so on?
- Do you find yourself comparing your children with each other and with others?
- Do you tend to help your kids because you do not want to see them "suffer" too much or struggle too hard?
- Have you ever apologized to your children and sought their forgiveness?
- Are you aware of some of the things you did that could stumble your children?

8

A Parent's Nightmare

The Lord heals the brokenhearted and binds up their wounds.

—Psalm 147:3 (NIV)

How thrilled I was when my daughter got accepted to her dream college! I thought I could breathe with a sigh of relief now that a big part of my mission as a parent was accomplished. My daughter would be able to start a brand-new life, living independently the way she anticipated. Empty-nest life would not be too bad for me at all, because my heart was filled with hope, joy, and pride!

Just when I thought everything was going well, I got a call from my daughter one day from school saying she had developed PTSD through a series of traumatic events. I could not believe what I heard when she shared all the details with me. The news hit me like a bolt out of the blue and made me feel cold and numb from my head to my toes.

I had no clue as to what PTSD was, how my daughter could get this disorder, how PTSD would affect her behavior, and how it could be treated. Questions, anger, sadness, fear, worry, and bitterness swirled restlessly around in my head. My heart raced and ached, but I had no tears, because I had to be strong for my daughter. I immediately blamed everyone else—including God— for putting her through so many painful trials in life. Yet in reality, I should be the one to be blamed the most because many of her agonies were built up little by little while she was still a child.

Like many parents, I thought I was loving my children unselfishly, unconditionally, and sacrificially because I was willing to do almost anything to help them succeed in life. Therefore, when I learned my daughter could not trust me or my love for her because of the hurt I inflicted on her, I was devastated. It was inconceivable to me that I contributed to much of my daughter's childhood pain, which culminated in the onset of PTSD.

As far as my daughter could remember, there was constant fighting between her dad and me as she was growing up. Following our legal separation, she was forced to adjust to the new family dynamics and make drastic changes in her living arrangement and school environment. The terminal illness and deaths of two loved ones in the family that took place within one year further added to her fear of loss and abandonment. On top of these family tragedies, she had to quietly endure various medical treatments and physical health challenges.

She had no say over the turmoil thrust upon her. Like wild grass that was dried up by the heat of the scorching sun, her sense of peace, security, stability, and identity was worn down by the cumulative effect of grief, helplessness, anxiety, and depression. When a sudden spark of trauma hit her, the dried grass instantly caught fire and started burning uncontrollably.

She told me once in high school that she felt like a Raggedy Ann doll that was broken and unloved, but I thought it was just a phase she was going through as a teen-ager. Surely everything would be wonderful as soon as she started college. She would be a new person with a new life. I had no idea about the danger lurking on a university campus, even one as prestigious and reputable as the one she was attending. I did not anticipate so many young people to be unbelievably lost and wild in college. I did not envision the problems of drugs, alcohol, sex, hazing, wild parties, attacks, assaults, stress, depression, suicidal attempts to be so prevalent and out of control.

Seeing my poor daughter struggling with PTSD overwhelmed me tremendously. Not comprehending what she was going through, or how to communicate with her when she was under a panic attack, made me feel totally inept and petrified. To show her my love, I avoided saying or doing anything that could agitate her. I also strained hard to keep an affirming composure and assuring tone of voice whenever I talked with her, in hope of helping her stay calm and bringing her comfort. Yet I could still somehow easily upset her when she was in the panic mode.

She tried to help me understand what was wrong with the way I loved her, but I simply could not get it. There were times when discouragement and defeat consumed me so much that I did not think I could make it. There were even times when I thought my daughter was just being vindictive and had made up her mind to punish me. At such times, I thought about just giving up trying to help her, but I could not, because she would always be my precious daughter.

Even though I seriously needed support and guidance from friends and family, I did not share much information with anyone. I did not think I could trust them to understand what we were going through. Fearing my daughter and I might be pitied, sneered at, or stigmatized in any way kept me from reaching out for help. I did not want people to feel sorry for us as helpless victims, and I wanted less for them to laugh at us.

Constant worrying made me quite paranoid about phone calls. When I did not get any calls or messages from my daughter for a few days, I worried. When the phone did ring, I panicked even more because I never knew what to expect from these calls. How I dreaded phone calls that came at odd hours during those few years. At the sound of the phone's ring, I was instantly on guard for the most alarming news.

Sure enough, in June 2009, my son answered an 11:00 p.m. phone call from China because I was still at a school board meeting. The call announced my dad's passing after being bedridden for fourteen months. Three months later, I was awakened by a phone call from my sister around 4:00 a.m., telling me our mom had also gone to the Lord in her sleep.

When it rains, it pours. As Chinese would say, "Piling frost on top of snow"—雪上加霜—*xue-shang-jia-shuang.* The trying days just seemed extra tough and long. With both my parents gone at almost the same time, I felt even more helpless and alone.

How could I be there for my daughter when I was in such miserable shape myself? I had already lost my husband and then my parents. I knew I did not want to also lose my daughter! I wished I could be with her to help her get well, but I could not. She was no longer a little girl living at home under my custody, and I did not know how to be a safe person for her. What could I do? What should I do?

I knew God would always listen to prayers, and the first thing I should do was to pray as taught in the book of Philippians 4: 6–7 (NIV): "Do not be anxious about anything, but in every situation, by prayer and petition, with thanksgiving, present your requests to God. And the peace of God, which transcends all understanding, will guard your hearts and your minds in Christ Jesus." However, I often tarried until I was at my wit's end and only turned to praying as my last resort.

In my desperation, I cried out to God for help. I prayed and prayed He would cure my daughter from PTSD and lead her out of the shadow of darkness.

Things to Think About:

- Do you think you have done a good job raising your children?
- Do you think a big part of your job as a parent is accomplished when your children are accepted to a good college?
- What experiences do you expect your children to get at college?
- What do you dread the most to see happening to your children?
- Do you care more about your children's doing than their being?
- Do you avoid facing relational, mental, and emotional health issues that you and/or your children might be having because of the fear of the stigma that might come with them?

9

Blessings in Disguise

And we know that in all things God works for the good of those who love Him, who have been called according to His purpose.

—Romans 8:28 (NIV)

There is a Chinese parable - *塞翁失馬,焉知非福* - *Sai-Weng-Shi-Ma,Yan-Zhi-Fei-Fu*. It is about a farmer who lost his one and only horse. All of the neighbors came by his house to extend condolences, but he said to them, "Not to worry, it may be a blessing in disguise." Sure enough, the horse came home a few days later with a mare, and the mare soon gave birth to a foal. This parable reminded me to look at the bad things that happen in life from a positive perspective. Each crisis in life may very well be God's opportunity!

By God's grace, through much prayer and meditation, it became more and more clear to me that God has a perfect plan for my daughter. I needed not worry so much about delivering her from her affliction, but to just trust Him to love my daughter more than

I could ever love her. I needed to learn to love my daughter in a way she could accept, and figure out what she was belaboring to express about the problem in our relationship.

It took me a long time to get what my daughter was trying to tell me, because my hearing was blocked by the cage of fear, pride, and self-righteousness. I was only able to hear what I wanted to hear. I picked and chose only her words that were agreeable with me. My acceptance of her was conditioned on her becoming the person I wanted her to be, even though I firmly believed what I wanted for her was good for her. Out of my pride I assumed I knew better, since I am her mom and, therefore, wiser. Out of my fear, I tried to shield her from any risks. I repeatedly put her down, though unintentionally, by my lack of trust in her ability to make her own decisions and be her own person. I thought I was protecting her out of love because I thought she was fragile and delicate, but I was stifling her growth.

How my daughter proved me wrong! She could not accept my so-called love for her or trust me as a safe person, because I tried too hard to show her what a good parent I was. She did not want to penalize me by holding me hostage to the past hurts I inflicted on her. She was not being ungrateful by refusing my offer to help her. She merely wanted me to give her space and time so that she could sort out her own problems and resolve them by herself.

By seeking conventional treatments as well as adopting holistic approaches through her studies in brain neurology and trainings in various therapies, my daughter was able to find ways to keep her PTSD under control. Not only did she find courage, strength, and wisdom in God to fight PTSD, she was also able to help some people who suffer PTSD and other mental health issues through her internship programs and church ministries.

Her transformation far surpassed my imagination and totally humbled and astounded me. I was moved and relieved to see her coming a long way to arrive at a place where she was able to develop confidence and peace within herself. At the same time, I was encouraged and inspired to also get well myself and break loose from my own cage.

Things to Think About:

- Do you tend to see the setbacks in life as stumbling blocks or stepping stones?
- Have you ever been surprised by what your children are capable of doing or becoming?
- Do you trust that God loves your children more than you could ever love them?
- Are there lessons that you could draw from observing or working with your children?
- Do you see blessings in some of your trying circumstances and/or hope in difficult relationships?

10

Overcoming Fear with Love

Love is not affectionate feeling, but a steady wish for the loved person's ultimate good as far as it can be attained.

— C. S. Lewis

There is no fear in love. Perfect love puts fear out of our hearts. People have fear when they are afraid of being punished. The man who is afraid does not have perfect love.

—1 John 4:18 (NLV)

It is truly by God's grace that my daughter's words were able to pierce through my cage to penetrate my heart and make me see the crux of my problem—I really did not know what love is or how to love. It is as if I have a love disorder.

What is wrong with my love? What is true love? How should I love? How could I work out a genuinely trusting, healthy, and loving relationship with my children and other people?

What Is Wrong with My Love?

I once heard an analogy that compared love to a bank account. Before withdrawing any money from the bank, deposits must be made. So where could I get deposits for my love bank? Since my marriage ended and both my parents passed away, my love bank account had been depleted. As a result, I found myself using a sort of counterfeit love, which had the appearance of love but lacked its value.

The counterfeit love deposits that would give me a sense of warmth and belonging were sometimes found by living vicariously through other people's lives, such as in dramas found in TV shows, movies, or novels and sometimes gained by social networking through a pseudo community. They were not love, but they were soothing and made me feel cozy at that moment. They were like foams and bubbles that filled the love bank quickly but would soon dissipate.

My love for my children and family was counterfeited in some ways, too. To avoid conflict, to stop causing more pain and hurt, to make up for my guilt, and to cover up my shame, I tiptoed around some issues to preserve superficial calm and peace.

Counterfeit love was also shown to some people I served. It was easy to give time, energy, and resources to help them because being charitable made me feel good about myself. Yet I was reluctant to give my true self to people lest they imposed on my personal and private life. I often gave the appearance of care, but the underlying purpose was to meet my own needs to be significant and fulfilled.

What Is True Love?

It was really timely when my pastor gave a sermon about true love based on the Disney animated movie *Frozen* just when I was searching for the meaning of true love. Pastor Paul quoted C. S. Lewis and elaborated, "Love is wanting the very best for someone and doing everything in our power to see it come about!"

What would be the very best for my children? I thought I was already doing all I could to give them the very best. However, after hearing the message, I knew I needed to examine more carefully as to whether my best was really the best for my children. If it was not, it could be toxic to them, like how Elsa, the elder sister in *Frozen*, froze the heart of Anna, her younger sister, to protect Anna from hastily marrying the wrong guy. To my regret, my love for my children had been toxic at times because it was out of the cage of fear, shame, guilt, insecurity, and pride.

If "only an act of true love can thaw [Anna's] frozen heart," then only an act of true love could heal the injured relationship between my daughter and me. Only with a truly unconditional and sacrificial love would I be able to break loose from the cage of fear to love not only my children but also myself and others freely and fully, because, "perfect love drives out fear" 1 John 4:18 (NIV).

Where Can I Find True Love?

I never thought I needed to struggle so hard to figure out where to find true love, because I took it as given that love would automatically exist between parents and children, husbands and wives, families and friends. Like most people, I regarded love as a warm and fuzzy feeling which was usually portrayed, dramatized, and sensationalized in films and books. However, 1 John 4:7–8 tells us that true love comes from God, because God is love. Out of my desperation to grasp true love, I decided I should study Bible more in depth because true love comes from God and He speaks to us through His Word.

To my surprise, I actually enjoyed studying His Word! I loved it so much that I even began to memorize verses. I also came to appreciate what was meant by the Chinese saying - 書中自有黃金屋—*shu-zhong-zi-you-huang-jing-wu* - Gold and riches could be found by reading books! Delving into the Holy Scriptures has turned out to be quite a gold-digging experience for me!

As I read the parable of the prodigal son in Luke 15, I learned about a father's love that was unselfish, unconditional, forgiving, gentle, patient, and generous. Even though his younger son ran away and squandered all the inheritance money he demanded from his father, the father never stopped loving him and waiting for his return patiently and longingly day after day. The father did not chase after his son or hover over him. He just let his son go, so he could learn his own lessons and make his own mistakes. When the son came home one day all filthy and broken, the father ran to greet his son while he was still a long way off. No harsh words. Just love, acceptance, and an embrace.

In John 4, I read about Jesus' compassion for an unworthy woman who had married multiple times, and was living with another man in a sinful lifestyle. She, a despised outcast tried to avoid being seen in public, so she was getting water from a well during high noon, when nobody else was around. What a surprise it was for her when she was addressed by Jesus, a respectable teacher of a higher social class. Not only was Jesus kind to her, He even offered her living water. This story gave me great hope to know that Jesus would not look down on me as a shameful person but would love me as He did the Samaritan woman.

My love bank account began to fill when I discovered substance, nourishment and strength through some of the teachings by Jesus and His apostles:

> "Fix your thoughts on what is true, and honorable, and right, and pure, and lovely, and admirable. Think about things that are excellent and worthy of praise. Keep putting into practice all you learned and received from me—everything you heard from me and saw me doing. Then the God of peace will be with you." Philippians 4: 8-9 (NLT)

> "Therefore do not worry about tomorrow, for tomorrow will worry about itself. Each day has enough trouble of its own." Matthew 6:34 (NIV)

> "Peace I leave with you; my peace I give you. I do not give to you as the world gives. Do not let your hearts be troubled and do not be afraid." John 14:27 (NIV)

"Be joyful always; pray continually; give thanks in all circumstances, for this is God's will for you in Christ Jesus." 1 Thessalonians 5: 16–18 (NIV)

The more I feasted on these gold nuggets of Bible verses the more deposits of joy, thanksgiving, peace, and love trickled into my love bank. On the contrary, the more I gave in to self-pitying, self-loathing and self-centeredness, the emptier my account got. When my love bank started to be filled by God's Word, not only would I find myself surrounded by more love, I would also have more love in my heart to give to others.

How can I live out this love?

How could I love effectively? How should I use my love deposits to invest in healthy relationships? The scriptures enlightened my eyes to see that only by the power of Holy Spirit would I be able to have hope, wisdom and ability to love authentically.

"For we know how dearly God loves us, because He has given us the Holy Spirit to fill our hearts with His love."Romans 5:5 (NLT)

"In the same way, the Holy Spirit helps us where we are weak. We do not know how to pray or what we should pray for, but the Holy Spirit prays to God for us with sounds that cannot be put into words." Romans 8: 26 (NLV)

> "Our hope comes from God. May He fill you with joy and peace because of your trust in Him. May your hope grow stronger by the power of the Holy Spirit." Romans 15:13 (NLV)

Further, I began to learn that love needs to be expressed and exercised within a loving and safe community where each member is held in respect, as well as being held accountable.

> "Live and work without pride. Be gentle and kind. Do not be hard on others. Let love keep you from doing that. Work hard to live together as one by the help of the Holy Spirit. Then there will be peace." Ephesians 4:2-3 (NLV)

> "Dear friends, since God loved us that much, we surely ought to love each other. No one has ever seen God. But if we love each other, God lives in us, and his love is brought to full expression in us. God so loved us, we also ought to love one another." 1 John 4:11–12 (NLT)

> "Just as our bodies have many parts and each part has a special function, so it is with Christ's body. We are many parts of one body, and we all belong to each other." Romans 12:4-5 (NLT)

> "Dear brothers and sisters, if another believer is overcome by some sin, you who are godly should gently and humbly help that person back onto the right path." Galatians 6:1 (NLT)

I tried to fill the emptiness in my soul with food, but it only led to a life-endangering addiction that brought shame and guilt. I tried to fill it with a desirable marriage, but it only led to heartbreak and disgrace. I tried to fill it with career success, but it only led to greed for more power, and I experienced more discontent. I tried to fill it by being a good parent, but it only made my children go through needless trials. Yet when God's love started to fill this void by the work of His Spirit and through a loving community, I began to sense peace, joy, and contentment in my heart and soul.

How do I apply the Book of Love in parenting?

To get a more comprehensive and practical understanding about true love, I looked up a very popular passage which is found in the Book of Love - 1 Corinthians 13: 4-8 (NIV):

> "Love is patient, love is kind. It does not envy, it does not boast, it is not proud. It does not dishonor others, it is not self-seeking, it is not easily angered, it keeps no record of wrongs. Love does not delight in evil but rejoices with the truth. It always protects, always trusts, always hopes, always perseveres. Love never fails."

1) *Be patient and kind*: The first thing I thought I should do was to learn to be patient and not to be quick to react and defend myself against any words directed at me that sounded critical. Even when I found some

remarks harsh and unbearable sometimes, I should empathize, observe, and listen with my heart to grasp the pent-up bitterness and pain behind such words. When I was able to put myself in my children's shoes and show grace, it would be more likely for us to build and fortify mutual trust and understanding.

2) *Be other-minded:* I also needed to put my children's welfare above my own ego, and that meant not to stir up strife just to prove my point, not to boast about how much and what I had done for them, not to pridefully think I knew it all, not to put them down when they did not do as I expected, not to justify my position for my own purpose, not to get angry at them easily, and not to keep score and hold a grudge against them. The goal is really not to win the debate but to build the relationship.

3) *Be truthful:* Learning to be truthful and not just agreeable is essential because it would be disingenuous on my part if I were simply patronizing to avoid confrontation. I should have a genuine desire in finding out my children's needs and interests so that I can work with them for their ultimate good, not just a temporary fix. I also should "speak in truth and in love" Ephesians 4:15 (NIV)

by being forthright and honest, yet gentle, compassionate, and empathetic.

4) *Be giving:* It is very important to give security, trust, and hope to my children, but I could only give them what I had. If I felt insecure or lacked hope, how could I give true security and hope to them? If I constantly hovered over my children, wouldn't I be demonstrating distrust to them? Even if I could not trust my children fully at times based on their own merits, I should always, "Trust in the Lord with all [my] heart and lean not on [my] own understanding" Proverbs 3:5 (NIV).

5) *Be persistent:* My love for my children should also be persistent and resolute. I should not be easily discouraged when things turned rough. Inspired by a message from Dr. Wendell Friest who ministered to the people in Taiwan for over forty years —I made a promise to my children that "there is nothing you could do that would ever stop me from loving you."

How Do I Communicate Love?

If love is expressed in an ineffective way or at an inopportune time, would it still be love? If love could not be felt by the targeted recipient, what good would that love be for that person?

In reading the book *The Five Love Languages* by Dr. Gary Chapman, published by Northfield Publishing Co., I was intrigued by the five languages that communicate love: words of affirmation, quality time, gifts, physical touch, and acts of service. If the love language spoken to the intended recipient is different from the love language that person receives, then love is not effectively communicated to that person. Therefore, I needed to figure out what love languages were spoken and received between my children and me.

When I read the parable of the prodigal son in Luke 15, I saw how the father expressed his love to each of his two sons differently. To the younger son who squandered all his money, the father showed his love by hugging him despite his stench and filth and giving him gifts and even a big feast after he returned home (i.e., physical touch and gifts). To the older son, who got really upset and jealous over his father's elaborate and lavish treatment of the younger son, the father kindly assured him all he had belonged to him (i.e., words of affirmation and gifts).

For me, acts of service would be my way of expressing love. The more I love a person, the more I would tend to do things for that person. It happened to work really well between my son and me because our speaking and receiving languages coincided. However, for my daughter, whose receiving love language was quality time and words of affirmation, it did not work so well. She could not sense my love when I kept doing things for her as acts of service. Even when I spoke her language by trying to affirm her with encouraging words or by spending quality time with her, it was not effective if I were not sincere with my words or if the time I spent with her was done as something to be checked off a to-do list.

My daughter helped me see that while it is essential to be effective in communicating love, it is far more important the love communicated is true. If my love for her or others is not genuine, then it would not matter if it is expressed in a proper or timely manner. The bottom line is that love must be true.

I was not able to love authentically, because I lacked true love for myself and others. I did not and could not love effectively, because my eyes were veiled and ears were dulled when I was too caught up with my own fear, shame, pride, insecurity, and guilt. While I knew that I should stop vacillating and meandering in and out of the cage, I could not do it on my own strength or willpower. Only by trusting and following the God of love who would set me free from the cage of fear and work in me could I love authentically and fully.

By learning to love, I have slowly arrived at a place where my children and I are able to share our hearts and minds with each other more openly and freely in love and in truth.

Things to Think About:

- Do you sometimes find your ears so clogged you cannot hear what your children are trying to say to you?

61

- Do you think you really know what love is or have experienced true love?
- Do you sometimes find it difficult to show and communicate love with your children or other people?
- Do you have people holding you accountable for the way you "love"?

11

From Cage to a New Page

> Therefore, if anyone is in Christ, the new
> creation has come: The old has gone, the new
> is here!
>
> —2 Corinthians 5:17 (NIV)

The process of coming out has not been easy because
it requires me to totally let go of everything I have
tightly clung to as my identity and security blanket,
and let God take control of my life. The process also
drags on because I often crawl right back to the cage
out of habit and familiarity, especially when things get
challenging. I have to keep reminding myself to trust
that God loves me with an infinite and forbearing love
that never fails, and He will do what He promises in
Jeremiah 29:11–14 (NIV).

> "For I know the plans I have for you," declares
> the Lord, "plans to prosper you and not to harm
> you, plans to give you hope and a future. Then
> you will call on me and come and pray to me,

and I will listen to you. You will seek me and find me when you seek me with all your heart. I will be found by you," declares the Lord, "and will bring you back from captivity."

Indeed, God has a distinct and unique plan for me as well as for my children, and we trust that His plan will prosper us, give us hope and give us a future. We also hold on to the promise that by "delight[ing] [ourselves] in the Lord, He will give [us] the desire of [our] heart" - Psalm 37:4 (NIV).

Seeing how much both my children have grown to love the Lord and choose to follow Him truly humbles me. Though they were stifled in multiple ways while growing up, by adults who were selfish, ignorant and busy, they have learned to overcome adversities in life by trusting God's provision and guidance with a thankful heart. As my son is attending law school on a full-ride scholarship right now, my daughter has found a part-time job developing curriculum for kindergarteners.

As for me, I am learning to "number [my] days, that I may gain a heart of wisdom," as admonished by Moses in Psalm 90:12 (NIV). How do I number my days? How would I know how long my life would be?

Looking at Moses' life on earth, it was evenly divided into three forty-years: the first forty being a self-righteous prince, the second forty being a meek shepherd, and the third forty being used as a powerful instrument in God's hand to lead Israelites out of Egypt.

I am in my mid-fifties now. I have lived my first twenty-six years striving for academic success, and my second twenty-six years pursuing parenting and career success. Well, I don't know if I have a third twenty-six years or how many more days I have on this earth, but I know I no longer want to seek personal success but be an instrument in God's hand to serve Him and others for His glory and purpose. I want to love myself, my children, family, friends, and other people the way God loves us.

By God's grace, I was given a new life and a new beginning as I embarked on my third journey in life. In 2012, not only was I totally cleared from cancer, I was given a clear vision to start a nonprofit organization to address the educational needs of our school district. God's love for me is just beyond words of description. Who am I to deserve such love, grace, and favor from Him?

My story does not end with a "happily ever after." I wish I could proclaim Romans 8:37 (NIV) and say, "[I am] more than conqueror through Him who loved [me]" all the time, but the truth is more like what apostle Paul experienced in Romans 7:24 and 15 (NIV): "What a wretched person I am!" "For what I want to do, I do not do, but what I hate, I do." I do not want to worry so much and frighten so easily, but I still do from time to time.

In moments when I get anxious, discontent, or caught up with people's opinion of me or my children, I have to remind myself, "I'm not trying to win the approval of people, but of God. If pleasing people were my goal, I would not be Christ's servant." Galatians 1:10 (NLT); and ask, "How foolish can you be? After starting your new [life] in the Spirit, why are you now trying to become perfect by your own human effort?" Galatians 3:3 (NLT).

I am excited about this new page in life because I now have confidence in knowing that "God is [my] refuge and strength, an ever-present help in trouble" Psalm 46:1 (NIV), so I do not need to hide in the cage anymore. I may still feel fear, shame, guilt, insecurity, and pride from time to time, but I don't need to dwell in them any longer, because "In God I trust, I will not be afraid," Psalm 56:4 (NIV).

With the many losses in relationships I have sustained in life—many of which resulted from my own ignorance, foolishness, egotism, selfish ambition, and vain conceit—I have now learned, "Unless the Lord builds the house [relationship, business, projects], the builders labor in vain" Psalm 127:1 (NIV). I need to give sovereignty to the Lord in all my relationships and endeavors, or I will just be wasting time and effort.

How am I going to live my next twenty-six days, twenty-six months, twenty-six or more years of life? Certainly not in a cage of fear any longer, because I do not want to pass any baggage on to my children, to their children, and to their children's children! I want to live out God's words by building a house of true love grounded on solid rock.

> "Therefore everyone who hears these words of mine and puts them into practice is like a wise

man who built his house on the rock. The rain came down, the streams rose, and the winds blew and beat against that house; yet it did not fall, because it had its foundation on the rock. But everyone who hears these words of mine and does not put them into practice is like a foolish man who built his house on sand. The rain came down, the streams rose, and the winds blew and beat against that house, and it fell with a great crash."Matthew 7:24–27 (NIV)

A Tiger Mom? I am certainly
not, so I thought.
A Tiger Mom! I've turned out
to be one, to my shock!
Out of a cage of fear, insecurity,
pride, shame, and guilt,
I raised my children with a love
that is toxic and flawed.

Come out of the cage, I must. I slowly walked.
Build a house of true love,
I will, on solid rock.
Into His word of truth and
wisdom, I searched
To live a life of love and faith
by His Spirit, I sought.

CPSIA information can be obtained at www.ICGtesting.com
Printed in the USA
LVOW11s1909180516

488875LV00001B/12/P